Ultimate Networking©
Workbook

George Edward Dubec

ISBN: 1983977640
ISBN 13: 9781983977640
Library of Congress Control Number: 2018901723
CreateSpace Independent Publishing Platform
North Charleston, South Carolina

Ultimate Networking Forms

YOU CAN GET ANYTHING YOU WANT BY NETWORKING

- Establish who and what you are in the marketplace and to others.

- Establish a clear, simple and concise message focusing on your main product, service, project or need. When completed, give to your referral network and others to help them, help you, find and get what you are looking for.........?

- A graphic illustration of the key elements involved in business networking.

- Assess yourself as a Business Networker to find out how you rate against the criteria established to be the best networker you can be; the "Ultimate Networker!"

- The checklist helps you to prepare in advance and network at peak efficiency.

- When you meet a qualified prospect, take good notes on this form. Detail action steps and time lines that you confirm with the prospect, for follow-up and follow-through.

Personal Brand (Template)

[WHO AND/OR WHAT ARE YOU?]

[TITLE / COMPANY NAME]

[BUSINESS CATEGORY]

[ONLINE]

- **[LINKEDIN]**
- **[FACEBOOK]**
- **[WEBSITE]**
- **[vCard (Virtual Business Card)]**
- **[Blog]**
- **[Newsletter]**
- **[SKYPE]**

[PRODUCTS / SERVICES / PROJECTS]

[ELEVATOR PITCH]

[UNIQUE SELLING PROPOSITION (USP)]

[OTHER]

Personal Brand (Example)

George Dubec - "Ultimate Networker"

Ultimate Networking

Consultant / Trainer / Coach / Public Speaker / Connector

Business Skills / Networking / Digital Marketing

ONLINE

- LINKEDIN - www.linkedin.com/in/georgedubec
- FACEBOOK – www.facebook.com/georgedubec
- WEBSITE – www.georgedubec.info
- WEBSITE – www.ultimatenetworking.info
- vCard – www.gd.123look.com
- vCard - www.ultimatenetworking.123look.com
- SKYPE – "georgedubec"

PRODUCTS / SERVICES / PROJECTS

- "Ultimate Networking" book
- "Reality Probe" (social interaction game - www.realityprobegame.com)
- Networking Skills Training / Coaching / Consulting
- Digital Marketing Training / Coaching / Consulting

   "I can show you how to get anything you want by networking"

- Over 50 years of Networking Experience
- Revolutionary Training with Performance Tracking
- Work with the "Ultimate Networker"

Networker Profile (Template)

[COMPANY / BUSINESS / PROJECT]

[NAME / TITLE]

[BACKGROUND]

[CREDIBILITY]

[PERSONAL / CONTACT INFO]

- [PHONE (W)]
- [PHONE (C)]
- [E-MAIL]
- [LINKEDIN]
- [FACEBOOK]
- [WEBSITE]
- [VIDEO]
- [VIRTUAL BUSINESS CARD]

[BUSINESS CATEGORY]

[PRODUCTS / SERVICES / PROJECTS]

[ELEVATOR PITCH]

[UNIQUE SELLING PROPOSITION (USP)]

[BENEFITS]

[REFERENCES]

[IDEAL REFERRAL]

[BUSINESS PLAN, EXECUTIVE SUMMARY OR TIMELINE]

[RESELLER, AFFILIATE OR REFERRAL PROGRAM]

[WHAT I NEED, WHAT I AM LOOKING FOR AND/OR IDEAL REFERRAL?]

Networker Profile (Example: BUSINESS)

COMPANY / BUSINESS / PROJECT: ULTIMATE NETWORKING

NAME: GEORGE DUBEC / "THE ULTIMATE NETWORKER"

TITLE: CONSULTANT, COACH, TRAINER, AUTHOR

BACKGROUND:
- FIFTY YEARS NETWORKING EXPERIENCE
- CORPORATE
- DIRECT SALES
- MLM / NETWORK MARKETING
- SOCIAL AND NETWORKING EVENTS / TRADE SHOWS
- ENTERTAINMENT
- FUND-RAISING / INVESTMENTS
- NONPROFITS / CHARITIES
- MATCHMAKING AND EVENTS FOR SINGLES
- ONLINE / SOCIAL MEDIA

CREDIBILITY:
- CORPORATE MANAGEMENT
- VP OF SALES AND MARKETING
- BUSINESS OWNER
- EVENT PLANNING FOR SOCIAL AND BUSINESS EVENTS, SEMINARS, WORKSHOPS, TRADE SHOWS
- BUSINESS NETWORKER AND CONNECTOR
- AUTHOR / TEACHER / TRAINER / COACH / CONSULTANT
- AFFILIATE MARKETER
- RADIO SHOW HOST AND PRODUCER

PERSONAL / CONTACT INFO:
PHONE (W): 561-777-3196
PHONE (C): 561-777-3196
E-MAIL: GEORGE@GEORGEDUBEC.COM
LINKEDIN: www.linkedin.com/in/georgedubec/
FACEBOOK: www.facebook.com/georgedubec
WEBSITE: www.georgedubec.info
VIRTUAL BUSINESS CARD: www.gd.vcardinfo.com
BUSINESS CATEGORY: NETWORKING / ONLINE MARKETING TRAINING
PRODUCTS / SERVICES / PROJECTS:
ULTIMATE NETWORKING BOOK / WEBINARS / GROUP and PRIVATE TRAINING

ELEVATOR PITCH
I am the "Ultimate Networker. I can help you get almost anything or everything you want by networking!"

UNIQUE SELLING PROPOSITION (USP):
- "Ultimate Networking" is a training platform that is unique and based on......
- Business Networking Rating System - How individuals rate against the criteria established to be the "Ultimate Networker" (the best of the best)
- Performance Tracking - Help you decide on what areas you need the most improvement and to make sure you implement the education and training
- Coaching, Training, Consulting - Provide the best education, principles, strategies, methods of operating and techniques to anyone who desires to become the "Ultimate Networker"
- Personal Branding - Market and promote to others who and what you are all about
- Referral Network - Help you get what you want and help others get what they want

BENEFITS:
- IMPROVE YOUR NETWORKING SKILLS USING PERFORMANCE TRACKING
- LEARN HOW TO GET MORE QUALIFIED LEADS
- LEARN HOW TO BUILD QUALITY RELATIONSHIPS AND A REFERRAL NETWORK
- FIND OUT HOW YOU RATE AS A BUSINESS NETWORKER
- ESTABLISH AN EFFICIENT SYSTEM FOR FOLLOW-UP AND FOLLOW THROUGH
- LEARN HOW TO USE THE NETWORKER PROFILE TO GET WHAT YOU WANT AND WHAT YOU NEED
- BECOME MORE ORGANIZED AND STRUCTURED
- IMPROVE COMMUNICATION SKILLS

REFERENCES:
- GEORGE K. (xxx-xxx-xxxx)
- MIKE O. (xxx-xxx-xxxx)
- CHARLIE T. (xxx-xxx-xxxx)
- ALAN L. (xxx-xxx-xxxx)
- KERRY B. (xxx-xxx-xxxx)

BUSINESS PLAN, EXECUTIVE SUMMARY, OR TIME LINE: No

RESELLER, AFFILIATE OR REFERRAL PROGRAM: 25 percent commission based on contract price

WHAT I NEED, WHAT I AM LOOKING FOR, AND/OR IDEAL REFERRAL
- BUSINESS OWNERS / SALES MANAGERS WHO WANT TO IMPROVE THE BUSINESS SKILLS OF THEIR STAFF AND EMPLOYEES
- SALES PEOPLE, BOTH NOVICE AND PROS, WHO WANT TO IMPROVE THEIR BUSINESS SKILLS
- NETWORK MARKETERS WHO WANT TO IMPROVE THEIR BUSINESS SKILLS
- CLUBS AND ORGANIZATIONS LOOKING FOR SPEAKERS
- RADIO AND TV SHOWS LOOKING FOR GUESTS WHO ARE EXPERTS IN THEIR FIELD

Networker Profile (Example: SOCIAL)

COMPANY / BUSINESS / PROJECT:
FINDING A MEMBER OF THE OPPOSITE SEX FOR MARRIAGE

NAME: JANE DOE

TITLE: PROFESSIONAL / MOTHER

BACKGROUND:

* AGE THIRTY-FIVE
* DIVORCED AFTER TEN YEARS of MARRIAGE
* TWO KIDS (GIRL NINE / BOY FIVE)
* OWNS A HOME IN BOCA RATON, FLORIDA
* 5' 6" / 125 POUNDS
* FIT AND IN GREAT SHAPE
* NONSMOKER
* SOCIAL DRINKER
* COLLEGE-EDUCATED
* FULL-TIME ACCOUNTANT
* LARGE FAMILY

PERSONAL / CONTACT INFO:
PHONE (W): XXX-XXX-XXXX
PHONE (C): XXX-XXX-XXXX
E-MAIL: myname@gmail.com
LINKEDIN: www.linkedin.com/in/janedoe
FACEBOOK: www.facebook.com/janedoe
VIRTUAL SOCIAL CARD – www.janedoe.com

ELEVATOR PITCH:

"Looking for a partner to share life and raise a family together. Open to someone that already has children or is intending to have more children."

UNIQUE SELLING PROPOSITION (USP):
Trustworthy, loyal, hard worker, and a good family person. Into health, fitness, and staying young

WHAT I NEED, WHAT I AM LOOKING FOR, AND/OR IDEAL REFERRAL

- MALE OVER 5' 10" WITH HAIR (PREFER DARK)
- NONSMOKER
- NO DRUGS OR ALCOHOL
- FIT AND IN SHAPE (NOT OVERWEIGHT)
- PROFESSIONAL
- NEVER MARRIED, DIVORCED, OR WIDOWED
- OK WITH HAVING CHILDREN
- DARK COMPLEXION
- DOES NOT TRAVEL OFTEN FOR WORK
- LIKES ALL TYPES OF MUSIC
- NONRELIGIOUS / NONPOLITICAL
- GOOD DANCER

Business Networker Infographic

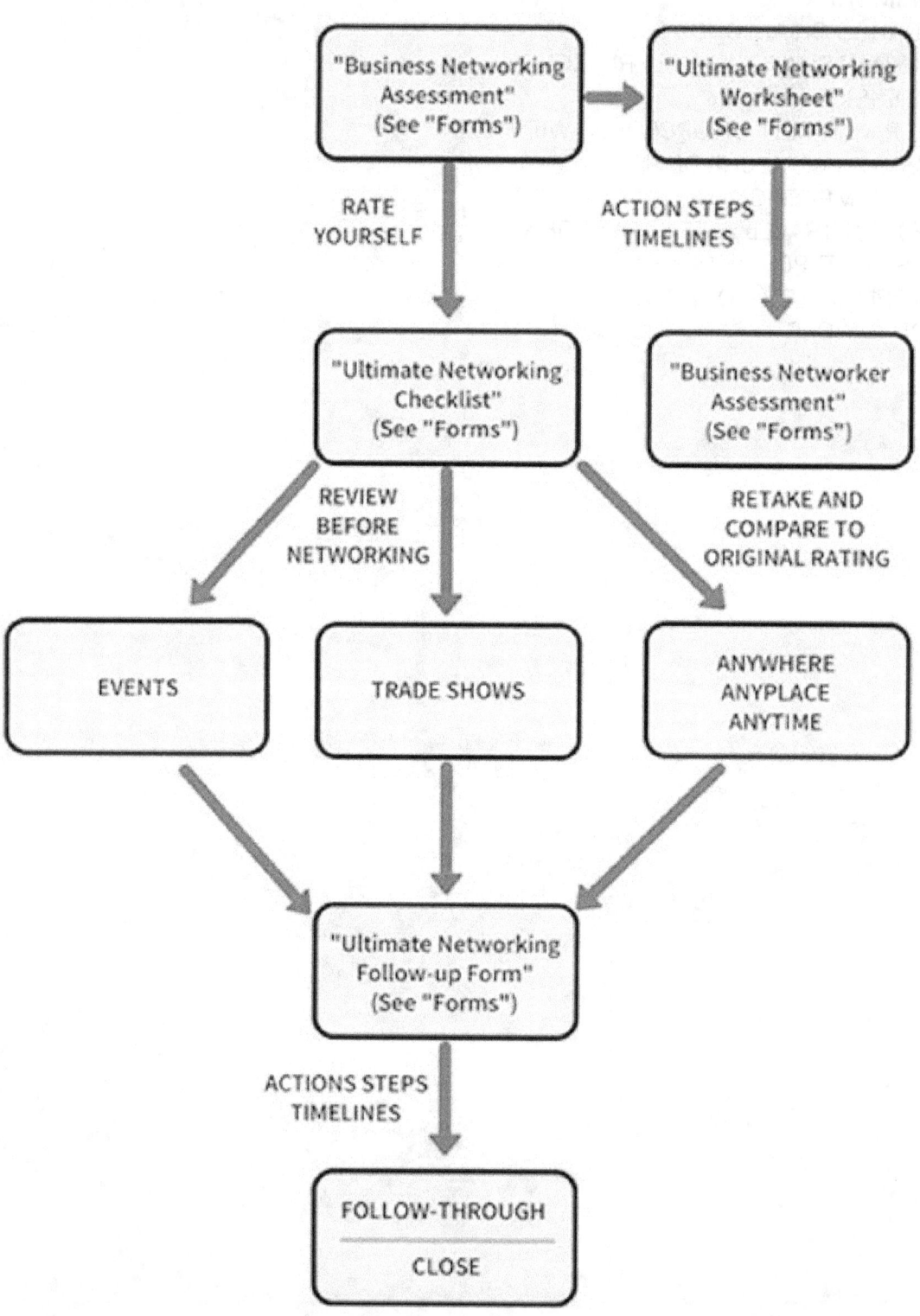

Business Networker Assessment

RATE YOURSELF AS A BUSINESS NETWORKER....

☐ Present rating as a Business Networker...scale of 1 to 10 (10 being high). Rate yourself on each point below ..... scale of 1 to 10 (10 being high). Circle your rating number on the scale as well as write in the appropriate box.

PREPARATION FOR NETWORKING

☐ 1. Establish your PERSONAL BRAND (see "FORMS")

```
0   1   2   3   4   5   6   7   8   9   10
```

☐ 2. Create a "Networker Profile" (see "FORMS")

```
0   1   2   3   4   5   6   7   8   9   10
```

☐ 3. Keep up to date on events in your area

```
0   1   2   3   4   5   6   7   8   9   10
```

☐ 4. Enjoy meeting new people and networking

```
0   1   2   3   4   5   6   7   8   9   10
```

☐ 5. Select events that will have prospects attending who are in your target market

```
0   1   2   3   4   5   6   7   8   9   10
```

☐ 6. Have a plan, establish your objectives and a time limit to spend at the event and with prospects

```
0   1   2   3   4   5   6   7   8   9   10
```

☐ 7. Invite friends, associates and customers to go to networking events with you

```
|__|__|__|__|__|__|__|__|__|__|
0   1   2   3   4   5   6   7   8   9   10
```

☐ 8. Find top networkers or salespeople in your category and ask them about their networking strategies

```
|__|__|__|__|__|__|__|__|__|__|
0   1   2   3   4   5   6   7   8   9   10
```

☐ 9. Have business cards, pen, notepad and/or a virtual business card (www. ultimatemobilemarketing.biz)

```
|__|__|__|__|__|__|__|__|__|__|
0   1   2   3   4   5   6   7   8   9   10
```

☐ 10. Rate the level of success of each of top 5 people you spend the most business time with each month on a scale of 1 thru 10 (10 being high). Then total the numbers of all 5 and divide by 5 to average the value of your business contacts

METHODS OF OPERATING

☐ 11. Create a name tag with your product or service displayed, along with your name

```
|__|__|__|__|__|__|__|__|__|__|
0   1   2   3   4   5   6   7   8   9   10
```

☐ 12. Meet with event promoter(s) and host(s) and ask for connections or referrals

```
|__|__|__|__|__|__|__|__|__|__|
0   1   2   3   4   5   6   7   8   9   10
```

☐ 13. Write legibly and complete all required information when filling in forms at networking events and trade shows

```
|__|__|__|__|__|__|__|__|__|__|
0   1   2   3   4   5   6   7   8   9   10
```

ULTIMATE NETWORKING WORKBOOK

☐ 14. Create special promotions, discounts, offers and rewards for your products and services with expiration dates to create a sense of urgency

```
|  |  |  |  |  |  |  |  |  |  |
0  1  2  3  4  5  6  7  8  9  10
```

☐ 15. Spend your time meeting new prospects; not talking to friends and associates at events

```
|  |  |  |  |  |  |  |  |  |  |
0  1  2  3  4  5  6  7  8  9  10
```

☐ 16. Verify the credibility of new prospects and associates, so as not to waste time

```
|  |  |  |  |  |  |  |  |  |  |
0  1  2  3  4  5  6  7  8  9  10
```

☐ 17. When being introduced, ask about the other person's business and how you can help them instead of talking about your products and services

```
|  |  |  |  |  |  |  |  |  |  |
0  1  2  3  4  5  6  7  8  9  10
```

☐ 18. Qualify prospects by asking their level of interest in your products, services or projects on a scale of 1 to 10 (10 being high)

```
|  |  |  |  |  |  |  |  |  |  |
0  1  2  3  4  5  6  7  8  9  10
```

☐ 19. Ask open-ended questions when conversing with newprospects

```
|  |  |  |  |  |  |  |  |  |  |
0  1  2  3  4  5  6  7  8  9  10
```

☐ 20. Pay compliments to those you meet and network with

```
|  |  |  |  |  |  |  |  |  |  |
0  1  2  3  4  5  6  7  8  9  10
```

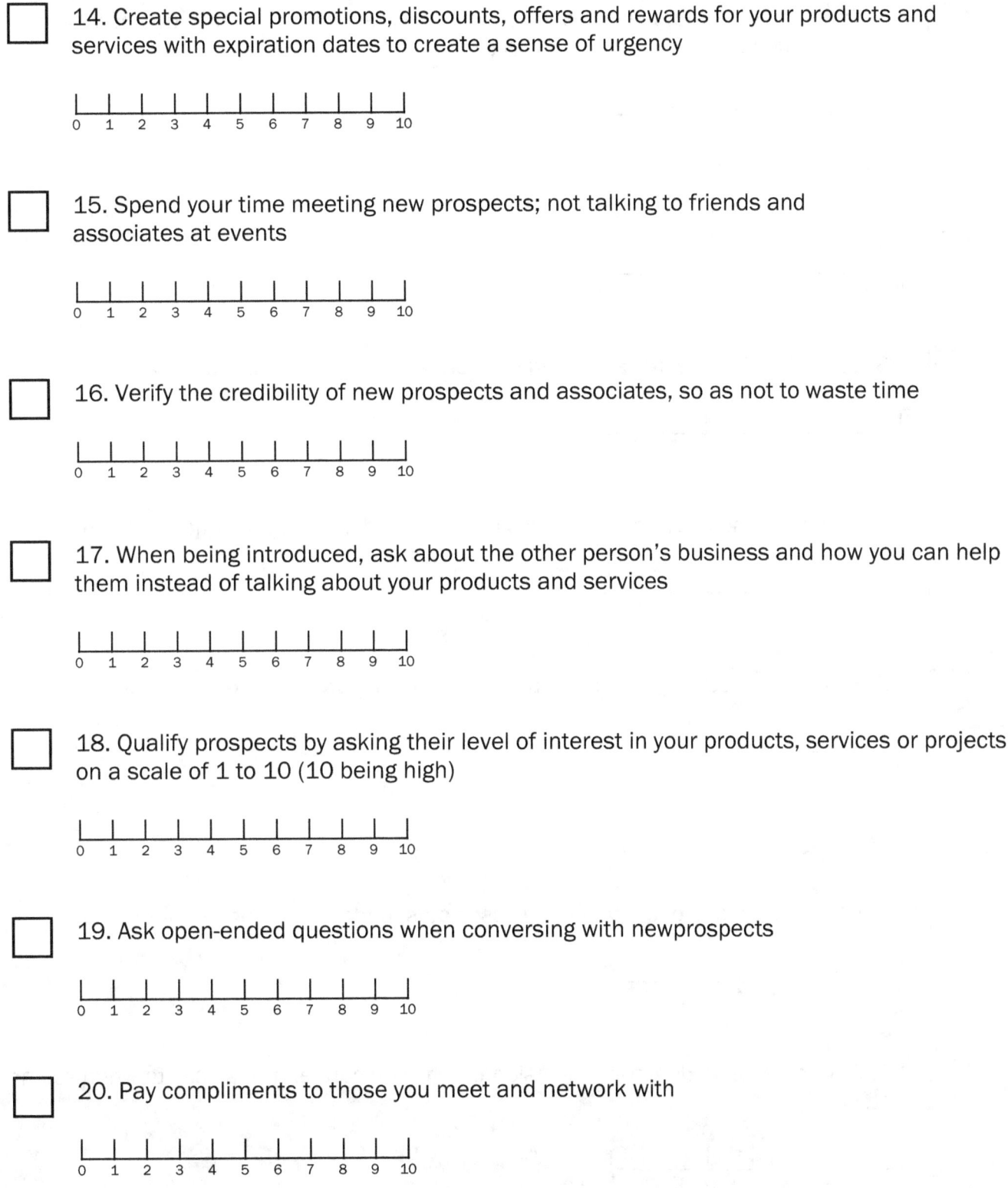

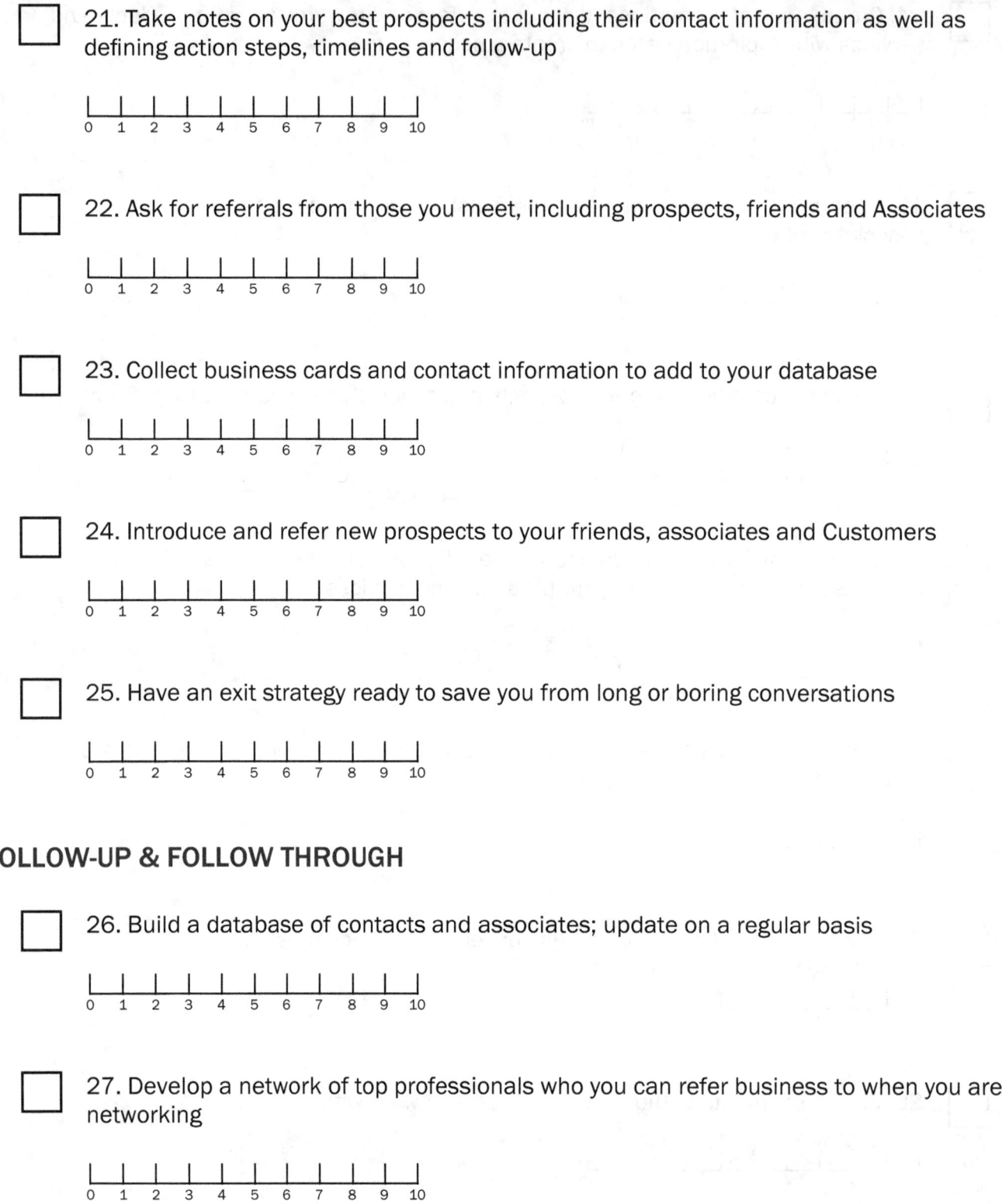

☐ 21. Take notes on your best prospects including their contact information as well as defining action steps, timelines and follow-up

```
|  |  |  |  |  |  |  |  |  |  |  |
0  1  2  3  4  5  6  7  8  9  10
```

☐ 22. Ask for referrals from those you meet, including prospects, friends and Associates

```
|  |  |  |  |  |  |  |  |  |  |  |
0  1  2  3  4  5  6  7  8  9  10
```

☐ 23. Collect business cards and contact information to add to your database

```
|  |  |  |  |  |  |  |  |  |  |  |
0  1  2  3  4  5  6  7  8  9  10
```

☐ 24. Introduce and refer new prospects to your friends, associates and Customers

```
|  |  |  |  |  |  |  |  |  |  |  |
0  1  2  3  4  5  6  7  8  9  10
```

☐ 25. Have an exit strategy ready to save you from long or boring conversations

```
|  |  |  |  |  |  |  |  |  |  |  |
0  1  2  3  4  5  6  7  8  9  10
```

FOLLOW-UP & FOLLOW THROUGH

☐ 26. Build a database of contacts and associates; update on a regular basis

```
|  |  |  |  |  |  |  |  |  |  |  |
0  1  2  3  4  5  6  7  8  9  10
```

☐ 27. Develop a network of top professionals who you can refer business to when you are networking

```
|  |  |  |  |  |  |  |  |  |  |  |
0  1  2  3  4  5  6  7  8  9  10
```

☐ 28. Establish a system to get referrals from customers, family, friends and associates (offer affiliate and reseller programs or other incentives)

```
|  |  |  |  |  |  |  |  |  |  |  |
0  1  2  3  4  5  6  7  8  9  10
```

☐ 29. Establish "Follow-up / Follow-Through" with a "Tickler File" system and Autoresponders

```
|  |  |  |  |  |  |  |  |  |  |  |
0  1  2  3  4  5  6  7  8  9  10
```

☐ 30. Follow-up with all qualified leads (within a couple of days)

```
|  |  |  |  |  |  |  |  |  |  |  |
0  1  2  3  4  5  6  7  8  9  10
```

☐ 31. Follow-through to close with all qualified leads after initial follow-up

```
|  |  |  |  |  |  |  |  |  |  |  |
0  1  2  3  4  5  6  7  8  9  10
```

☐ 32. Return all phone calls, answer all e-mails and text messages from new contacts expressing your level of interest in their products or services on a scale of 1 to 10 (10 being high). Then follow-up asking their level of interest in your products and services plus ask for a referral

```
|  |  |  |  |  |  |  |  |  |  |  |
0  1  2  3  4  5  6  7  8  9  10
```

☐ 33. Put in the time, effort, discipline, training and practice to improve your "Business Networker Assessment" score

```
|  |  |  |  |  |  |  |  |  |  |  |
0  1  2  3  4  5  6  7  8  9  10
```

RATING

_____ TOTAL (of SCORES above) _____ AVERAGE (divide TOTAL by 33) = Business Assessment

Rating Rank yourself as follows ....1 to 4 ....Weak (need help). 5 to 8.....Average (doing OK, but could do better). 9 or 10...Strong (getting good results)

Ultimate Networking Checklist

☐ 1. Establish your Personal Brand (see "FORMS") as it relates to your main products, services, and projects

☐ 2. Complete a "Networker Profile" (see "FORMS")

☐ 3. Select a networking event, conference or trade show that fits your target market

☐ 4. Plan the strategies and techniques which you will be using to accomplish your networking goals and objectives

☐ 5. Invite a friend, customer or associate to attend with you (optional)

☐ 6. Business cards, smartphone, pen, notepad and your virtual business card (www.ultimatemobilemarketing.biz)

☐ 7. Dress appropriately to fit the event

☐ 8. Collect any and all the business cards you can (to input to your database) at networking events, expos and trade shows from   sponsors, exhibitors, attendees as well as hosts and promoters

☐ 9. Meet the event host(s) or promoter(s) and ask them if they can connect you with anyone who might be interested in your products and services

☐ 10. Qualify prospects (those interested in your products and   services). Ask what level of interest they have for your products, services or projects on a scale of 1 to 10 (10 being high)?

☐ 11. Have an opening line ready and follow with some casual conversation upon an introduction

☐ 12. Ask open-ended questions and listen twice as much as you speak!

☐ 13. Say your prospects name often and pay compliments

☐ 14. Have your "Elevator Pitch" and "USP (Unique Selling Proposition)" prepared

☐ 15. Take good notes and prepare to define action steps and timeline on a clipboard or in a notebook for follow-up

☐ 16. Ask about other's products and services, then inquire as to what they are looking for and if you can help them?

☐ 17. Ask for referrals

☐ 18. Have an exit strategy to leave unproductive discusions and meetings?

☐ 19. Establish a follow-up system

☐ 20. Establish a follow-through system (includes "TICKLER" file autoresponders)

Ultimate Networking Worksheet

ULTIMATE NETWORKING WORKSHEET			
STRATEGIES/TECHNIQUES	ACTIONS STEPS	TIMELINE	RATING

Ultimate Networking Follow-Up Form

ULTIMATE NETWORKING FOLLOW-UP FORM				
NAME/COMPANY	CONTACT INFO	REASON FOR INTEREST	ACTION STEPS/TIMELINE	PRIORITY

Performance Tracking Infographic

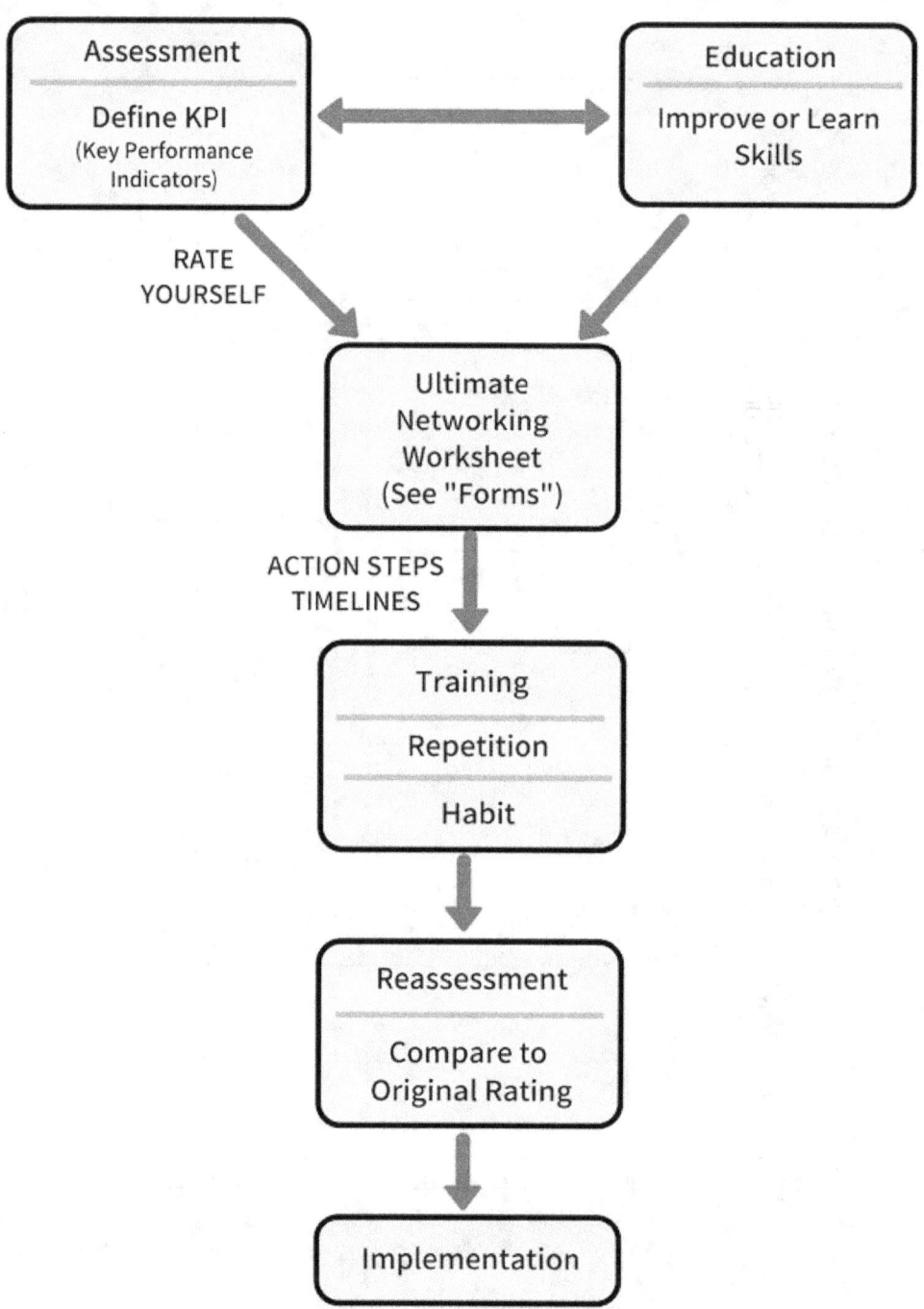

Performance Tracking for Personal Motivation

GOALS & OBJECTIVES

_____Have a defined goal, objective, project or business on a scale of 1 to 10 (10 being high)

Scale 1 to 3 (just thinking about it)

Scale 4 to 6 (have an idea; getting started with fact-finding, planning and action steps)

Scale 7 or 8 (off the ground but need help with time, resources, funding to get it done)

Scale 8 or 9 (moving forward with some minor obstacles in my way)

Scale 10 (on fire; nothing is going to stop me)

_____How many hours per week can you devote to your project?

SELF-IMPROVEMENT

_____Desire to become better on a scale of 1 to 10 (10 being high)

Scale 1 to 4 (need some improvement)

Scale 5 to 7 (status quo, not much motivation)

Scale 8 or 9 (ready to get on fire)

Scale 10 (on fire)

_____How many hours per week can you devote to self-improvement?

AREAS FOR SELF-IMPROVEMENT

Rate each category below from 1 to 10 (10 being high) as to your level of competency

_____Business Networking

_____Health

_____ Finances

_____ Weight

_____Relationships

_____ Social Life

_____Entertainment

_____Sports

_____Family

_____Public Speaking

_____Sales

_____Self-Image

_____Education

_____People Skills

_____Time Management

_____Other

HOW ARE YOU GOING TO ACHIEVE SUCCESS

Input a percentage in each selected category; totaling 100%

_____Self-Motivation

_____Hire coach, trainer, consultant

_____Education from books, webinars, seminars, workshops

_____Connect with others such as mentors, business partners, investors, mastermind groups

Referral Directory Infographic

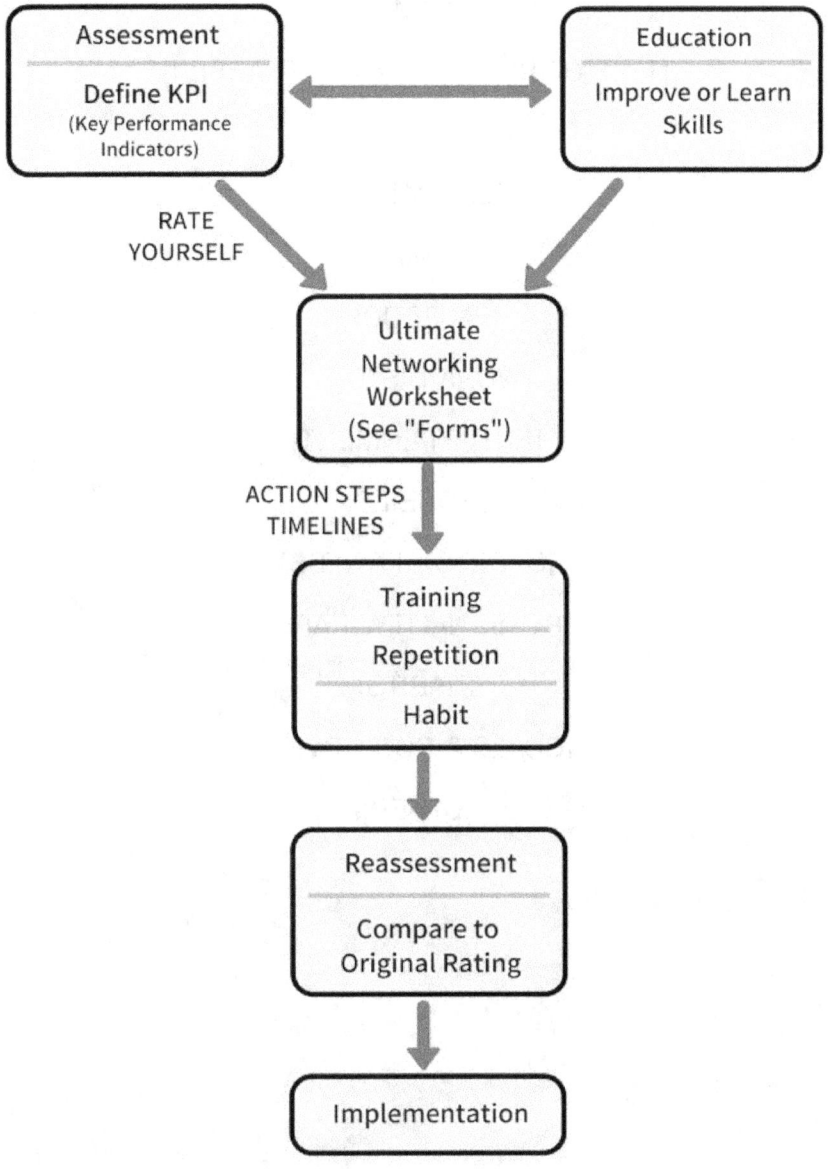

Personal Interview (Template)

[NAME]

[TYPE OF BUSINESS / JOB / CAREER]

[BACKGROUND]

[EDUCATION]

[FAMILY]

[FACEBOOK]

[WORK HISTORY]

[ENTERTAINMENT]

[HOBBIES]

[SPORTS / FITNESS]

[PERSONALITY TRAITS]

[HABITS]

[GOALS & OBJECTIVES]

[OTHER]

Personal Interview (Example)

George Dubec / DOB – 1946

Ultimate Networking

Consultant / Trainer / Coach / Public Speaker / Connector

Youngstown, Ohio 1946 / Boardman, Ohio 1950 / Warren, Ohio 1970 / Boca Raton, Florida 1985

BSBA - Youngstown State University

FAMILY

- Divorced once / married - 38 years
- Three kids - Cara (25) / Mark (47) / Suzy (50)
- Three grandkids - Taylor (20) / Luke (16) / Grace (13)
- One great grandkid - Ava (1 year)

FACEBOOK - www.facebook.com/georgedubec

WORK HISTORY

- Engineer (General Motors) - 18 years
- FAM Network - Business Owner (social events & dating) - 5 years
- VP of Sales & Marketing (Interaxx TV Network) - 2 years
- VP of Sales & Marketing (WebStream & Securenet Systems) - 15 years
- Entrepreneur / Consultant / Connector - 7 years

ENTERTAINMENT / HOBBIES / FITNESS

- Workout daily - swim, cross fit, weights, machines
- Work on my projects
- Family time
- Networking

PERSONALITY TRAITS

- Hard worker / Honest with integrity / Friendly / Helpful / Connector / Realist

GOALS & OBJECTIVES

- "Ultimate Networking" book
- "Ultimate" book series
- Reform education, politics, family life and the human condition

Life Networking Infographic

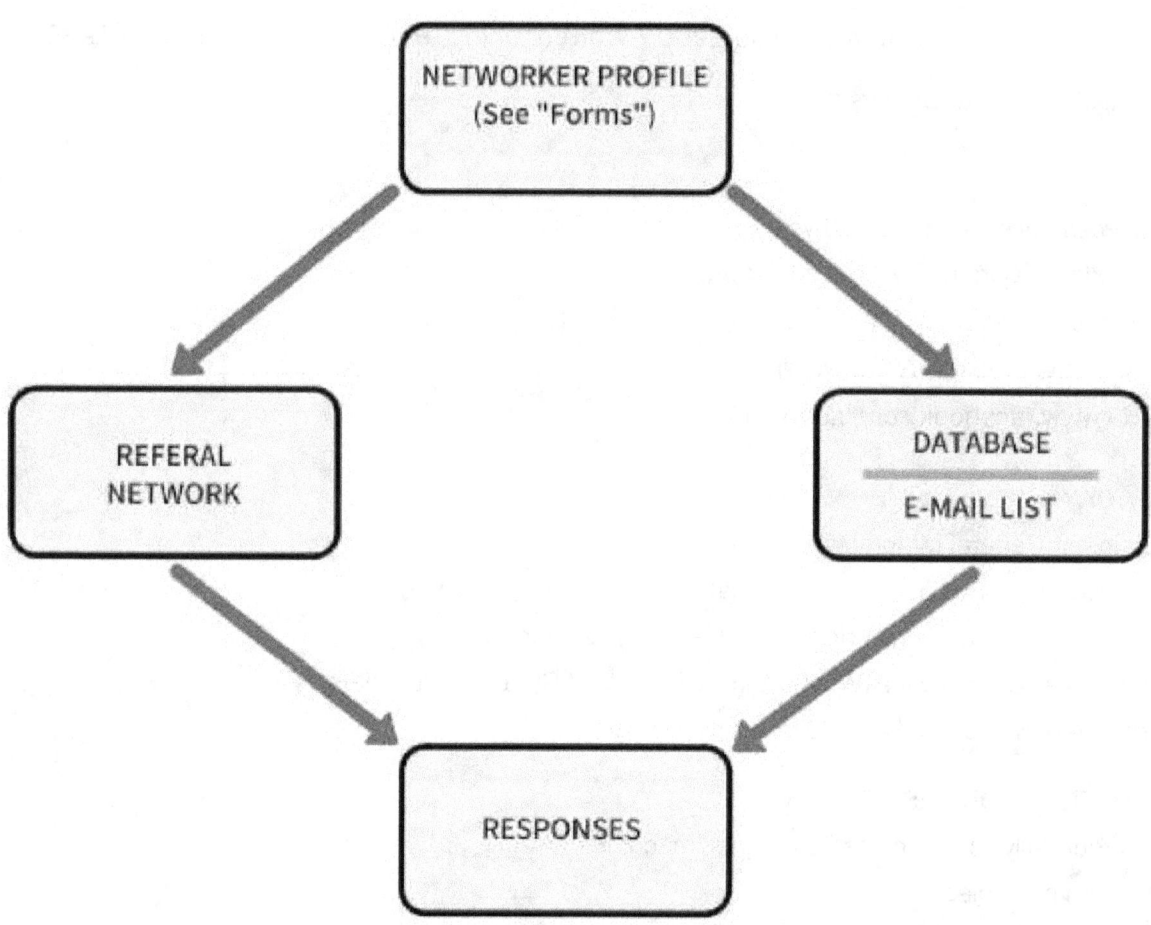

By The Numbers

The numbers and statistics below are not to be construed as verified by the scientific research, but rather indicators to be used to make better decisions on your work efforts and time.

1. ..... [1] **INDICATOR OF SUCCESS**

   - 15% based on skill and technical knowledge
   - 85% based on the ability to interact with people and build relationships

2. ..... [2] **READING AND MEMORIZATION**

   - One-third of high school graduates never read another book for the rest of their lives.
   - 42 percent of college graduates never read another book after college.
   - 80 percent of U.S. families did not buy or read a book last year.
   - 70 percent of U.S. adults have not been in a bookstore in the last five years.
   - 57 percent of new books are not read to completion.

3. ..... [3] **SUCCESS WITH SYSTEMS AND COURSES**

   - Less than 10% of people actually succeed with any system, method or course.

4. ..... [4] **BEST WAY TO ACQUIRE CUSTOMERS**

   - 85 percent said word-of-mouth referrals
   - 2 percent said radio ads
   - 1 percent said newspaper ads
   - 9 percent said Google/Facebook ads
   - 2 percent said direct mail

5. ..... [5] **SALES STATISTICS**

   - 48% of sales people never follow-up with a prospect.
   - 25% of sales people make a second contact and stop.
   - 12% of sales people only make three contacts and stop.
   - 10% of sales people make more than three contacts.
   - 2% of sales are made on the first contact.
   - 3% of sales are made on the second contact.
   - 5% of sales are made on the third contact.
   - 10% of sales are made on the fourth contact.
   - 80% of sales are made on the fifth to twelfth contact.

6. ..... [6] **STATISTICS ON HOW MUCH WE REMEMBER**

- WE REMEMBER 5% of what we get from a lecture.
- 10% of what we read
- 20% of what we see
- 30% of what we get from a demonstration
- 50% of what we see, hear and discuss
- 70% of what we say and write
- 80% of what we experience, practice and do
- 90% of what we teach others

7. ..... [7] **SIX DEGREES OF SEPARATION**

- 29% are able to make a connection

8. ..... [7] **NETWORKING**

- 91.4% of business owners said networking is part of their success
- 88 % of business owners never had a course on networking

9. ..... [8] **HABITS OF THE WEALTHY**

- 88% of the wealthy believe relationships are a key factor in their wealth. Only 17% of the poor agree.
- 67% of the rich believe promoting yourself is important to success. Only 24% of the poor agree.
- 75% of the rich send thank-you cards or notes or email regularly. Only 13% of the poor have this Rich Habit.
- 72% of the wealthy volunteer five hours or more each month compared to only 12% for the poor.

[1] *How to Win Friends and Influence People* by Dale Carnegie

[2] http://mentalfloss.com/article/27590/who-reads-books

[3] *Milana Leshinsky's Simplicity Circle* (www.milana.com/blog/ there-is-no-guru)

[4] Alignable recently completed a survey of 7,500 small-business owners in North America

[5] National Sales Executive Association

[6] Edgar Dale plus the Learning Pyramid from the NTL Institute, Bethel, Maine

[7] *Networking Like a Pro* by Misner & Hilliard (Entrepreneur Press, 2017)

[8] *Rich Habits* by Tom Corley - Relationship Building Archives - Rich Habits Institute)

RECOMMENDED READING

"56 Sales Statistics You Must Know in 2017 & Beyond" (https://getcrm. com/blog/sales-statistics/)